The Usborne
First Atlas

This edition first published 2012. First published in 2003 by Usborne Publishing Ltd,
Usborne House, 83–85 Saffron Hill, London, EC1N 8RT, England.

www.usborne.com

Title page: A satellite image showing rivers joining the sea, along the coast of
Guinea-Bissau in west Africa. The red parts are land and the blue parts are water.
This page: These mountains and glaciers are on the island of Svalbard, which belongs
to Norway. The island is far inside the Arctic Circle and it's very cold there.

The Usborne
First
Atlas

Elizabeth Dalby

Designed by Laura Hammonds,
Candice Whatmore and Ruth Russell

Digital imagery by Keith Furnival

Edited by Kirsteen Rogers

Cover design: Steve Moncrieff

Consultant: John Davidson

Cartography: European Map Graphics Ltd

Consultant cartographic editor: Craig Asquith

Usborne Quicklinks

The Usborne Quicklinks Website is packed with links to the best websites on the internet. To find links for this book, go to:

www.usborne.com/quicklinks
and enter the keywords "first atlas"

You'll find links to websites where you can:
• Zoom into satellite images of Earth
• Take a photo tour of the Amazon Rainforest
• See the view from the top of Mount Everest
• Find out about the everyday lives of people around the world
• Try map games, puzzles and activities

Internet safety guidelines
When using the internet please follow the internet safety guidelines displayed on the Usborne Quicklinks Website.

The recommended websites in Usborne Quicklinks are regularly reviewed and updated, but Usborne Publishing Ltd is not responsible for the content or availability of any website other than its own. We recommend that children are supervised while using the internet.

Contents

These brightly painted
houses are in Buenos
Aires, the capital city
of Argentina in
South America.

Rio Grande

Mississippi

Central America

Gulf of
Mexico

Cuba

Caribbean Sea

About maps

An atlas is a collection of maps.
Maps are pictures of areas, seen
from above. They show places
much smaller than they really
are. Some maps show the
whole world, and some
show much smaller
areas, like cities
or streets.

Guiana
Highlands

Amazon

Amazon Rainforest

SOUTH
AMERICA

Andes

Atacama Desert

Pampas

Patagonia

Cape Horn

What will you
see on a map?

Maps should be easy to
understand. Different kinds
of shading and symbols help
show what a place is like. A key
explains what they all mean.

The size of a map compared
with the real-life area it shows is
called its scale. Some maps have
a line called a scale bar that
shows you the real distances
between places on the map.

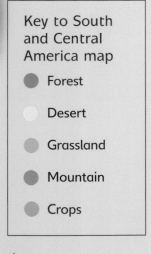

Key to South
and Central
America map

● Forest

○ Desert

● Grassland

● Mountain

● Crops

This map shows what
the land in South and
Central America is like.

Scale

Scale bar ——

| 0km | 2,000km |
| 0 miles | 1,240 miles |

Which way is up?

The Earth doesn't really have a top and
a bottom. Maps are often drawn with
north at the top, though, to make them
easier for everyone to understand.

This compass symbol
shows which way is
north (N), south (S),
east (E) and west (W).

Sea and land

More than two-thirds of the Earth is covered in salty water – the seas and oceans. Maps usually show water in blue.

The rest of the Earth is covered in land. Maps sometimes shade the land as it would look from above. Grasslands are often green and deserts can be sandy brown or yellow.

An island is land with water all around it. This is one of the Solomon Islands, in the Pacific Ocean.

Countries and continents

The land is divided into seven huge areas called continents, which are split into smaller areas called countries. Each country is run by a government and has its own laws. Some large countries are further divided into states, to make them easier to run.

Internet links

For links to websites where you can zoom into satellite images of the Earth, go to **www.usborne.com/quicklinks**

This is the continent of North America. It is a large area of land and islands.

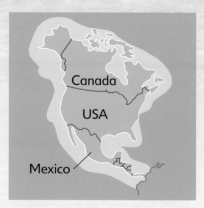

North America is divided into countries, including Canada, the USA and Mexico.

The USA is divided into 50 different states. Each state can make its own laws.

7

Information from maps

Maps can show different things about the same area. Some maps show where countries and cities are. Some show what the land looks like or what kinds of plants grow there.

Political maps show countries and place names. The lines between countries are called borders or boundaries.

Physical maps show what the land looks like. They show features like mountains, lakes and rivers.

Thematic maps show other information, such as what the land is used for, or how many people live there.

Weather and wildlife

Different parts of the world have their own weather patterns, plants and wildlife. These areas are called biomes. Deserts, grasslands and rainforests are biomes. They can all be shown on a thematic map.

These cacti live in the desert, where it hardly ever rains. They store water in their stems.

Internet links

For links to websites where you can find map games and puzzles, go to **www.usborne.com/quicklinks**

How many people?

The people who live in an area are its population. Maps can be used to show which parts of an area are crowded, and which parts have very few people living in them.

This map of North America shows the areas where most people live.

Key
people in each
km² (0.39 sq miles)

- None
- Fewer than 1
- Up to 100
- More than 100

Towns and cities

Anywhere where a group of people live is called a settlement. A village is a small settlement, a town is bigger, and the largest kind is a city. The capital city of a country is where its government is based. About half the people in the world live in a town or a city.

Lines on maps

To make it easy to measure distances and find places on a map, the Earth is divided up with imaginary lines. The two sets of lines are called longitude and latitude. They are numbered in degrees (°) and minutes (´).

Lines of latitude run around the globe. On maps they usually run from left to right.

Longitude lines run from the North to the South Pole, and usually from top to bottom on maps.

This drawing of the Earth shows the North Pole and the main lines of longitude and latitude.

North Pole

Lines of latitude

Arctic Circle (66°30´N)

Prime Meridian Line (0°)

Tropic of Cancer (23°27´N)

Equator (0°)

Tropic of Capricorn (23°27´S)

Lines of longitude

This globe is tipped slightly forward so the North Pole shows. This means that you can't quite see the South Pole.

The world's land

This is a physical map. It shows the different kinds of land in each continent.

The top half of the globe is called the northern hemisphere.

The bottom half of the globe is called the southern hemisphere.

Arctic Circle

Alaska
Mount McKinley ▲
Beaufort Sea
Victoria Island
Queen Elizabeth Islands
Ellesmere Island
Baffin Island
Baffin Bay
Greenland
Greenla
Aleutian Islands
Gulf of Alaska
Mackenzie
Great Bear Lake
Hudson Bay
Labrador Sea
Iceland
British Isles

NORTH AMERICA

Rocky Mountains
Yukon
Missouri
Great Plains
Lake Superior
Lake Michigan
Lake Huron
Appalachian Mountains
Newfoundland
Azores

Rio Grande
Colorado
Mississippi
Atlas Mo

Tropic of Cancer

Hawaiian Islands
Central America
Gulf of Mexico
Cuba
West Indies
Caribbean Sea
Canary Islands
S a

20° N

Cape Verde Islands

Equator

PACIFIC
OCEAN
Galapagos Islands
Guiana Highlands
ATLANTIC
OCEAN

P o l y n e s i a

Amazon
Amazon Rainforest
SOUTH AMERICA

Andes
Atacama Desert

Tahiti

20° S

Tropic of Capricorn

Aconcagua ▲
Paraná

Easter Island

Pampas

Patagonia

Falkland Islands

South Georgia

Cape Horn
Drake Passage

60°

Antarctic Circle
Antarctic Peninsula
Weddell Sea

80°

Vinson Massif ▲

160° 140° 120° 100° 80° 60° 40° 20° W

10

Key to map of the world's land

- ● Forest
- ● Grassland
- ○ Desert
- ● Mountain (only high mountains are shown)
- ○ Tundra (frozen ground with no trees)
- ○ Ice (areas where the ice or snow never melts)
- ● Crops (land used for growing plants for people and animals to eat)
- ○ Sea
- ● Lake or inland sea
- — River
- ▲ Mountain peak

Scale

0km	3,000km
0 miles	1,860 miles

ARCTIC OCEAN

Svalbard
North Cape
Novaya Zemlya
Barents Sea
andinavia
Kara Sea
Severnaya Zemlya
Laptev Sea
New Siberia Islands
East Siberian Sea
Arctic Circle

UROPE
Danube
Black Sea
Mount Elbrus ▲
Caspian Sea
Volga
Ural Mountains
Ob
Yenisey
Aral Sea
Altai Mountains
Siberia
Verkhoyansk Range
Lena
Lake Baikal
Amur
Sea of Okhotsk
Bering Sea
Kamchatka Peninsula
60°

ASIA
Gobi Desert
Sea of Japan
Japan
Honshu
40°

Mediterranean Sea
Libyan Desert
Nile
Arabia
Red Sea
Rub al Khali (Empty Quarter)
Himalayas
Indus
Ganges
Mount Everest ▲
Yangtze
Hwang
China
East China Sea
Taiwan
PACIFIC
Tropic of Cancer

esert
h e l
Arabian Sea
India
Bay of Bengal
Mekong
Luzon
Philippines
South China Sea
Micronesia
OCEAN
20° N

AFRICA
Ethiopian Highlands
Cape Comorin
Sri Lanka
Mindanao
Equator

Lake Victoria
Kilimanjaro ▲
ongo
Seychelles
Sumatra
Borneo
Celebes
Java Sea
Java
New Guinea
Mount Wilhelm ▲
Solomon Islands
Melanesia

Comoro Islands
Zambezi
Madagascar
Mauritius
INDIAN
OCEAN
Arafura Sea
Coral Sea
Great Barrier Reef
New Caledonia
Fiji Islands
20° S

Namib Desert
Great Sandy Desert
Tropic of Capricorn

ape of Good Hope
OCEANIA
Great Victoria Desert
Great Dividing Range
Tasman Sea
North Island
40°

Kerguelen Islands
Tasmania
New Zealand
South Island

60°

SOUTHERN OCEAN
Antarctic Circle

ANTARCTICA
Ross Sea
80°

Countries of the world

This is a political map. It shows the different countries that make up each continent. Can you find your country on the map?

GREENLAND
(Denmark)

ICELAND

NC

DEN

IRELAND UNITED
KINGDOM N

BE

FRAN

ALASKA
(U.S.A.)

Arctic Circle

CANADA

60°

80°

SPAIN

PORTUGAL

Azores
(Portugal)

UNITED STATES
OF AMERICA

40°

MOROCCO

Canary Islands
(Spain)

ALGE

WESTERN SAHARA
(Morocco)

Tropic of Cancer

THE BAHAMAS

20°
N

MEXICO

CUBA

DOMINICAN
REPUBLIC

HAITI

MAURITANIA

MALI

Hawaiian
Islands
(U.S.A.)

BELIZE

JAMAICA

CAPE VERDE

SENEGAL

GUATEMALA HONDURAS

Caribbean Sea

DOMINICA

THE GAMBIA

BURKINA
FASO

EL SALVADOR NICARAGUA

GUINEA-BISSAU

GUINEA

BEN

COSTA RICA

TRINIDAD AND TOBAGO

SIERRA LEONE

TOGO

PANAMA

VENEZUELA

GUYANA

IVORY
COAST

LIBERIA

GHANA

PACIFIC

COLOMBIA

SURINAME

FRENCH GUIANA
(France)

EQUATO
GU

0° Equator

Galapagos Islands
(Ecuador)

ECUADOR

SAO TOME AND
PRINCIPE

OCEAN

ATLANTIC

KIRIBATI

PERU

BRAZIL

OCEAN

Cook
Islands
(New Zealand)

French
Polynesia
(France)

BOLIVIA

20°
S

Tropic of Capricorn

Pitcairn
Islands
(U.K.)

PARAGUAY

CHILE

URUGUAY

ARGENTINA

40°

Falkland Islands
(U.K.)

South Georgia
(U.K.)

SOUTHER

60°

Antarctic Circle

Weddell
Sea

80°

160° 140° 120° 100° 80° 60° 40° 20° W

12

Key to map of countries of the world

— Border, where one country is joined to the next one

— Coast

● Lake or inland sea

Some country names had to be shortened to fit on the map. This list has the names written in full.

ARM. Armenia
AUST. Austria
AZER. Azerbaijan

BELG. Belgium
B.H. Bosnia and Herzegovina
CRO. Croatia
CZECH REP. Czech Republic
K. Kosovo
LEB. Lebanon
LUX. Luxembourg

MAC. Macedonia
M. Montenegro
NETH. Netherlands
SLOV. Slovenia
S. Serbia
SWITZ. Switzerland
U.A.E United Arab Emirates

Scale

| 0km | 3,000km |
| 0 miles | 1,860 miles |

ARCTIC OCEAN

RUSSIA

EN FINLAND
ESTONIA
LATVIA
SSIA LITHUANIA
LAND BELARUS
NY
REP. UKRAINE
SLOVAKIA MOLDOVA
JNGARY ROMANIA
.H.S.
M. K. BULGARIA
MAC. Black Sea
ANIA GEORGIA
GREECE ARM. AZER.
TURKEY
CYPRUS SYRIA
LEB.
ISRAEL IRAQ
JORDAN
KUWAIT
BAHRAIN
QATAR
U.A.E.

KAZAKHSTAN

Caspian Sea
UZBEKISTAN KYRGYZSTAN
TURKMENISTAN TAJIKISTAN
AFGHANISTAN
PAKISTAN

MONGOLIA

CHINA

NORTH KOREA
SOUTH KOREA
JAPAN

PACIFIC OCEAN

80°
60°
40°

Arctic Circle

terranean Sea

.IBYA EGYPT

SAUDI ARABIA
OMAN

NEPAL BHUTAN
BANGLA-DESH
INDIA
BURMA (MYANMAR)
LAOS
THAILAND
VIETNAM
CAMBODIA

Tropic of Cancer
20° N

CHAD SUDAN
ERITREA YEMEN
DJIBOUTI

PHILIPPINES

Northern Mariana Islands (U.S.A.)

MARSHALL ISLANDS

CENTRAL AFRICAN REPUBLIC
ROON
SOUTH SUDAN
ETHIOPIA
UGANDA
KENYA
SOMALIA

SRI LANKA
MALDIVES

BRUNEI
MALAYSIA
SINGAPORE

PALAU

FEDERATED STATES OF MICRONESIA

Equator 0°

CONGO (DEMOCRATIC REPUBLIC)
O
RWANDA
BURUNDI
TANZANIA

SEYCHELLES

INDIAN OCEAN

INDONESIA

NAURU

KIRIBATI

SOLOMON ISLANDS

TUVALU

COMOROS

EAST TIMOR (TIMOR-LESTE)

PAPUA NEW GUINEA

GOLA ZAMBIA MALAWI
ZIMBABWE MADAGASCAR MAURITIUS
BIA BOTSWANA MOZAMBIQUE
Reunion (France)

Coral Sea Islands Territory (Australia)

VANUATU

New Caledonia (France)

SAMOA

FIJI TONGA
20° S

Tropic of Capricorn

SWAZILAND
SOUTH AFRICA LESOTHO

AUSTRALIA

40°

NEW ZEALAND

Kerguelen Islands (France)

CEAN

60°

Antarctic Circle

ANTARCTICA

80°

E 40° 60° 80° 100° 120° 140° 160° 180°

North America

This continent includes three huge countries – Canada, the USA and Mexico. It also includes the Caribbean islands and the countries in the strip of land that joins onto South America.

Key to North America map
- ■ Capital city
- ○ Major city or town
- ━ Border (where one country joins another one)
- ─ River
- ▬ Coast

Scale

0km	1,000km
0 miles	620 miles

PACIFIC OCEAN

Raccoons live in North and Central America. They usually sleep in trees during the day and come out at night to feed.

Internet links

For links to websites with quizzes on North America and maps to print, go to **www.usborne.com/quicklinks**

ARCTIC OCEAN

Queen Elizabeth Islands

Arctic Circle

Bering Strait

Point Barrow

Beaufort Sea

ALASKA
(U.S.A.)

Parry Islan

Bering Sea

Yukon

Mount McKinley ▲

○ Anchorage

Victoria Island

Gulf of Alaska

Mackenzie

Great Bear Lake

CANAD

Great Slave Lake

Lake Athabasc

Reindeer Lake

○ Calgary

○ Vancouver

Winni

○ Seattle

Missouri

Columbia

Great Plains

Great Salt Lake

UNITED STATE

California

San Francisco

Colorado

○ Denver **(U S**

Hawaiian Islands
(U.S.A.)

Los Angeles

○ Phoenix

Lower California

Ciudad Juarez

Tex

○ Hermosillo

Rio Gran

Tropic of Cancer

Monterrey ○

MEXIC

○ Guadalaja

■ Mexico City

○ Acapulco

GREENLAND
(Denmark)

Greenland is part of North America, but it belongs to Denmark, in Europe.

Arctic Circle

Baffin Bay

Baffin Island

Nuuk

Cape Farewell

Labrador Sea

Hudson Bay

Labrador Peninsula

Newfoundland

St. John's

Quebec

St. Lawrence

Nova Scotia

nnipeg

Lake Superior

Quebec

Halifax

Montreal

Ottawa

Lake Huron

Lake Ontario

Boston

nneapolis

Toronto

Appalachian Mountains

ake Michigan

Detroit

Lake Erie

New York

Chicago

Pittsburgh

Philadelphia

s City

St. Louis

Cincinnati

Washington, D.C.

Ohio

Arkansas

Mississippi

ATLANTIC

OCEAN

Cape Hatteras

· *Bermuda*
(U.K.)

Atlanta

Florida

ouston

New Orleans

Tropic of Cancer

Miami

THE BAHAMAS

Nassau

Gulf of Mexico

Havana

Puerto Rico
(U.S.A.)

ST. KITTS AND NEVIS

DOMINICAN REPUBLIC

ANTIGUA AND BARBUDA

Guadeloupe (France)

CUBA

HAITI

DOMINICA

Martinique (France)

Merida

Port-au-Prince

Santo Domingo

ST. LUCIA

BARBADOS

racruz

Yucatan Peninsula

JAMAICA

Kingston

ST. VINCENT AND THE GRENADINES

GRENADA

BELIZE

Belmopan

Caribbean Sea

TRINIDAD AND TOBAGO

GUATEMALA

HONDURAS

Port-of-Spain

Guatemala City

Tegucigalpa

San Salvador

NICARAGUA

EL SALVADOR

Managua

San Jose

Panama City

COSTA RICA

PANAMA

This photograph was taken from space by a satellite. The orange parts are deserts. The brown areas are the Rocky Mountains.

North America facts

Total land area 24,709,000km² *(9,540,198 sq miles)*

Biggest country Canada 9,984,670km² *(3,855,103 sq miles)*

Smallest country St. Kitts and Nevis 261km² *(101 sq miles)*

Biggest island Greenland 2,166,086km² *(836,330 sq miles)*

Highest mountain Mount McKinley, Alaska, USA 6,194m *(20,321ft)*

Longest river Mississippi/Missouri, USA 6,019km *(3,740 miles)*

Biggest lake Lake Superior, USA/Canada 82,414km² *(31,820 sq miles)*

Highest waterfall Yosemite Falls, California, USA 739m *(2,425ft)*

Biggest desert Great Basin Desert, USA 492,000km² *(189,962 sq miles)*

Using the land

Much of the land in North America is hard to live and work on. Some areas are hot and rocky, and some are freezing and snowy. In other parts of North America, the land and weather are just right for farming.

Shapes in the rock

In the southwest USA, some of the rocky land has slowly been worn away by rivers to make channels called canyons. Strong winds and rain have worn the rock away even more, making strange, rippling shapes.

The Great Lakes

This map shows some types of land in North America.

Key

● Snow and ice

● Mountains and deserts

● Grasslands and forests

● Farmland

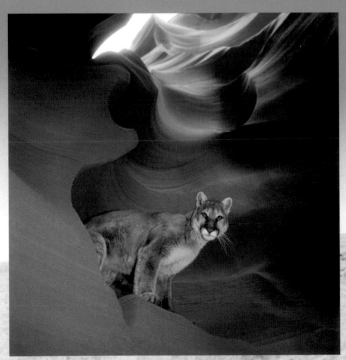

This strange photograph shows part of a small canyon in Arizona. The orange rock is called sandstone and the big cat is a puma.

Shaking ground

The Earth's crust is made up of huge slabs of rock, called plates. Sometimes they push or slide against each other, making the ground shake. This is called an earthquake. The San Andreas Fault, in the west of the USA, is a place where two plates slide past each other. Earthquakes often happen there.

This house fell down after a big earthquake in San Francisco, a city on the San Andreas Fault.

Massive farms

In the USA, Canada and Mexico, there are many huge cattle farms, called ranches. The cattle are farmed for their meat and skins. Other farms in North America grow crops such as corn and vegetables in enormous fields.

Internet links

For links to websites where you can explore the Grand Canyon and other American landscapes, go to **www.usborne.com/quicklinks**

One of the best ways for cowboys to move around their land and round up cattle is on horseback. Some farms are so big it would take days to walk across them.

Cities and celebrations

Explorers from Europe arrived in North America a few hundred years ago. But people have lived there for many thousands of years. Today, people come from all over the world to live there.

Stone cities

The Maya and the Aztec people lived in Mexico before European settlers came. The Maya built beautiful cities and pyramid-shaped temples out of stone. Ruins of these can still be seen today, on the Yucatan Peninsula in Mexico.

This map shows where some early North American people lived.

Key

● Aztecs

● Maya

● Native American tribes

Inuit

Inuit

Chipewyan

Cree

Inuit
Cree

Blackfoot

Chippewa

Chinook

Crow

Cheyenne

Huron

Cherokee

Comanche

Sioux

Iroquois

Hopi

Creek

Chickshaw

Navajo

Chocktaw

Apache

Yucatan Peninsula

This Mayan temple is over 1,000 years old.

The Maya believed their kings were gods and built temples like this one to worship them.

Busy city

New York City is the biggest city in the USA, and also one of the largest cities in the world. Over 8 million people live there, and thousands more visit every year.

Internet links

For links to websites where you can take virtual tours of North American cities and explore ancient sites, go to **www.usborne.com/quicklinks**

Part of New York is on an island called Manhattan. Bridges join Manhattan to the rest of the city.

Icy homeland

Inuit people live in the icy north of Canada, in an area called Nunavut. It's too cold to grow crops there, so Inuit hunters catch animals and fish for people to eat.

This boy has just caught a fish while ice fishing. He cut a hole in the frozen lake to fish through.

Calypso music

People visit the Caribbean islands for warm weather and sandy beaches. The islands are also famous for calypso music, which people play on drums made out of old oil cans.

This girl is dressed for Trinidad's carnival. Dancing and music are an important part of the celebrations.

South America

South America stretches down from the equator almost as far as the Antarctic. It is joined to North America by a narrow strip of land at the edge of Colombia.

Key to South America map
- ■ Capital city
- ○ Major city or town
- —— Border (where one country joins another one)
- —— River
- ▨ Coast

Scale
0km	1,000km
0 miles	620 miles

Caribbean Sea

Maracaibo
■ Caracas
VENEZUELA
Medellin
■ Bogota
Guiana Highla
Cali
COLOMBIA
Orinoco

Equator
Negro

Galapagos Islands (Ecuador)
Quito
ECUADOR
Amazon
Guayaquil

Amazon Rainfores
Ma
PERU
Ucayali
A N D E S

Lima
Lake Titicaca
BOLIVIA
La Paz
Atacama Desert
■ Sucre

Tropic of Capricorn

PACIFIC
CHILE
San Migu de Tucun
A N D E S

OCEAN
Cordoba
Aconcagua
Rosa
Santiago ■
ARGENTINA
Pamp

This is a toucan. Toucans live in South American rainforests. They use their long beaks to pick and eat fruit from the trees.

Patagonia

Strait of Magellar
Tierra del Fueg
Cape Horn
Drake Passa

Georgetown
'ANA ■ Paramaribo
URINAME ■ Cayenne
FRENCH GUIANA
(France)

ATLANTIC

OCEAN

na Reservoir
Amazon Belem
aus *Xingu*
Equator

Fortaleza
Tucurui Reservoir

B R A Z I L

Sobradinho Reservoir

Recife

Plateau of Mato Grosso

Tocantins
Sao Francisco
Brazilian Highlands

Salvador

■ Brasilia
○ Goiania

○ Belo Horizonte

Parana
Furnas Reservoir

RAGUAY
Sao Paulo ○ Rio de Janeiro
Tropic of Capricorn
■ Asuncion

○ Curitiba

○ Porto Alegre

ATLANTIC

URUGUAY
■ Montevideo
OCEAN
Buenos Aires

alkland Islands
(U.K.)

This is what South America looks like from space. The mottled strip along the west coast shows the Andes Mountains.

Internet links

For links to websites with South America maps to print, go to **www.usborne.com/quicklinks**

South America facts

Total land area *17,840,000km²*
(6,888,063 sq miles)

Biggest country Brazil *8,514,877km²*
(3,287,612 sq miles)

Smallest country Suriname *163,820km²*
(63,251 sq miles)

Biggest island Tierra del Fuego *47,401m²*
(18,302 sq miles)

Highest mountain Aconcagua, Argentina *6,962m (22,841ft)*

Longest river Amazon, Brazil *6,800km*
(4,225 miles)

Biggest lake Lake Maracaibo, Venezuela *13,210km² (5,100 sq miles)*

Highest waterfall Angel Falls, on the Churun River, Venezuela *979m (3,212ft)*

Biggest desert Patagonian Desert, Argentina *670,000km²*
(258,688 sq miles)

Wettest and driest

South America has one of the wettest places on Earth in it – the Amazon Rainforest. But it also has the Atacama Desert, which is one of the driest. South America's Andes Mountains make up the the longest chain of mountains in the world.

Snowy peaks

The Andes Mountains are over 7,000km (4,300 miles) long, and stretch all the way down the continent. The lower slopes are good for farming, but the high peaks are snowy and bleak. More than 30 of the peaks in the Andes are volcanoes.

This climber is close to the top of Huascaran, one of the highest peaks in the Andes.

This map shows some of the landscape features of South America.

Key

Amazon Rainforest

Rivers in the Amazon

Atacama Desert

Andes Mountains

Forest homes

The Amazon Rainforest is the biggest rainforest in the world. It's always hot there and it rains nearly every day. The forest is home to a huge number of plants and animals.

This blue morpho butterfly comes from the Amazon. It's as big as a man's hand.

Internet links

For links to websites with photo tours of the Amazon Rainforest and the Andes Mountains, go to **www.usborne.com/quicklinks**

Dry ground

The Atacama Desert, in Chile, is next to the Pacific Ocean but it is the driest place on the planet. In some parts of the desert, people think it may never have rained at all.

Desert plants like these have long roots to reach way down into the cracked earth for water.

Mighty river

There's more water in the Amazon River than in any other river in the world. Over 1,000 smaller rivers flow into it, from all over the north part of South America. It is also one of the longest rivers, and winds nearly all the way across the top of the continent.

This boy is paddling his boat along the Amazon River. The main part of the river is so wide there are no bridges over it.

Places for living

South Americans live high in the mountains, deep in the rainforest, and even in the desert. Many people live in tiny farming villages, but South America also has some of the biggest cities in the world.

This map shows the places where most people live in South America.

Key
people in each km²
(0.39 sq miles)

- None
- Fewer than 1
- Up to 100
- More than 100

The Uros people use boats made of reeds to cross Lake Titicaca.

Mountain lake

Lake Titicaca is high up in the Andes Mountains, near Peru and Bolivia. The Uros people live by the lake and go fishing in its icy waters. Some of them live on floating islands made of reeds.

Mysterious statues

Easter Island, in the Pacific Ocean, is covered in hundreds of stone figures called *moai*. They were made by the first people who lived there, to worship their ancestors.

Most *moai* statues are at least twice the height of a man, and very heavy. How they were moved into place is a mystery.

City celebration

Early every year, the busy city of Rio de Janeiro in Brazil holds a carnival. It lasts for five days, with feasting, music and costume parades. Dancers take part in samba competitions across the city.

At carnival time in Rio de Janeiro, floats like this one carry costumed people through the streets of the city.

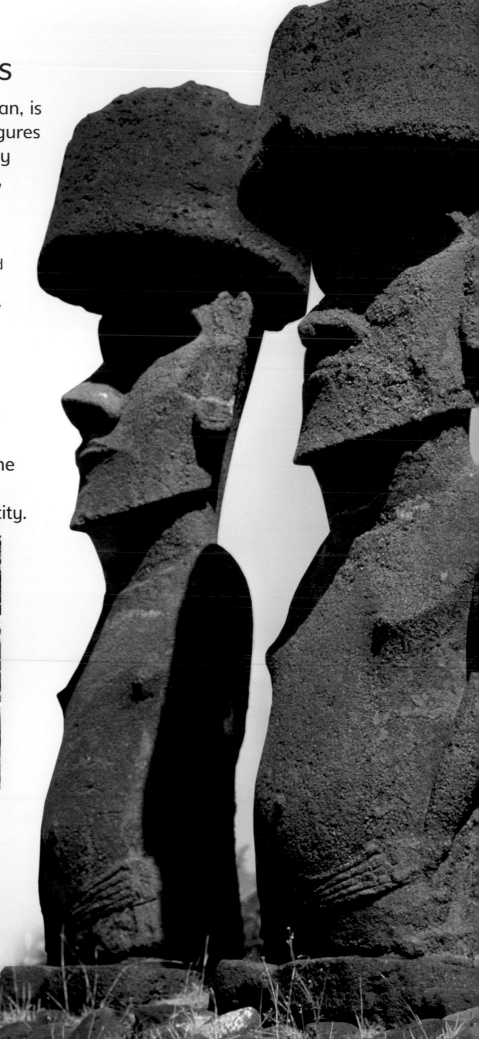

Internet links

For links to websites where you can learn more about South America, go to **www.usborne.com/quicklinks**

Asia

Asia is the biggest continent. It stretches from the Arctic Circle to the equator, and from the Ural Mountains in the west to the Pacific Ocean in the east.

ARCTIC OCEAN

The part of Russia on this side of the Ural Mountains is in Europe.

Novaya Zemlya

Barents Sea

Kara Sea

No

Arctic Circle

Arkhangelsk

St. Petersburg

Yenisey

■ Moscow

Nizhniy Novgorod

Kazan

Ural Mountains

Ob

R U S

Yekaterinburg

Irtysh

Ob

Volga

Samara

Chelyabinsk

Omsk

Novosibirsk

Istanbul

Black Sea

Rostov

Astrakhan

Aqtobe

■ Astana

Altai Mounta.

Izmir

Ankara

Caucasus Mountains

Caspian Sea

KAZAKHSTAN

TURKEY

GEORGIA

Tbilisi

Aral Sea

Lake Balkhash

Nicosia

ARMENIA

Yerevan

CYPRUS

AZERBAIJAN

Baku

Urumqi

Beirut

SYRIA

UZBEKISTAN

Almaty

Key to Asia map

- ■ Capital city
- ○ Major city or town
- ▬ Border (where one country joins another one)
- ╱ River
- ▰ Coast

LEBANON

Damascus

Tigris

Tabriz

TURKMENISTAN

Ashgabat

Bishkek

ISRAEL

Euphrates

Tashkent

KYRGYZSTAN

Jerusalem

Amman

Baghdad

Tehran

Dushanbe

JORDAN

IRAQ

Mashhad

TAJIKISTAN

Syrian Desert

IRAN

Kunlun Mount.

Basra

AFGHANISTAN

Islamabad

Plateau of Tibet

KUWAIT

Kabul

H I M A L A Y A S

Lh.

Scale

0km	1,000km
0 miles	640 miles

Medina

SAUDI ARABIA

Shiraz

Kandahar

PAKISTAN

Delhi

NEPAL

Jedda

Indus

Mount Evere

Mecca

BAHRAIN

Riyadh

The Gulf

QATAR

New Delhi

Kathmandu

BHUTA

Red Sea

Abu Dhabi

Thar Desert

Ganges

UNITED ARAB EMIRATES

Muscat

Karachi

Varanasi

BANGLADESH

Rub al Khali (Empty Quarter)

Nagpur

Dhaka

OMAN

Kolkata (Calcutta)

Sana

YEMEN

Arabian Sea

Mumbai (Bombay)

INDIA

Bay of Beng

Aden

Socotra (Yemen)

Giant pandas live in bamboo forests in the high mountains of west China. These days, there are fewer than 2,500 giant pandas left in the wild.

Bangalore

Chennai (Madras)

SRI LANKA

Cape Comorin

Sri Jayewardenepura Kotte

Colombo

MALDIVES

■ Male

Equator

Internet links

For links to websites with maps of Asia to print, go to **www.usborne.com/quicklinks**

INDIAN OCEAN

The white ridges across the middle of this satellite photograph of Asia are the snowy peaks of mountain ranges.

Asia facts

Total land area
44,537,920km² (17,196,187 sq miles)

Biggest country Russia
Total area: 17,075,200km² (6,592,772 sq miles) Asiatic Russia: 12,780,800km² (4,934,694 sq miles)

Smallest country Maldives
300km² (116 sq miles)

Biggest island Borneo
748,168km² (288,869 sq miles)

Highest mountain Mount Everest, Nepal/China 8,848m (29,029ft)

Longest river Yangtze (Chang Jiang), China 6,380km (3,964 miles)

Biggest lake Caspian Sea, western Asia 370,999km² (143,244 sq miles)

Highest waterfall Jog Falls, India 253m (830ft)

Biggest desert Arabian Desert (deserts of Saudi Arabia) 2,330,000km² (900,000 sq miles)

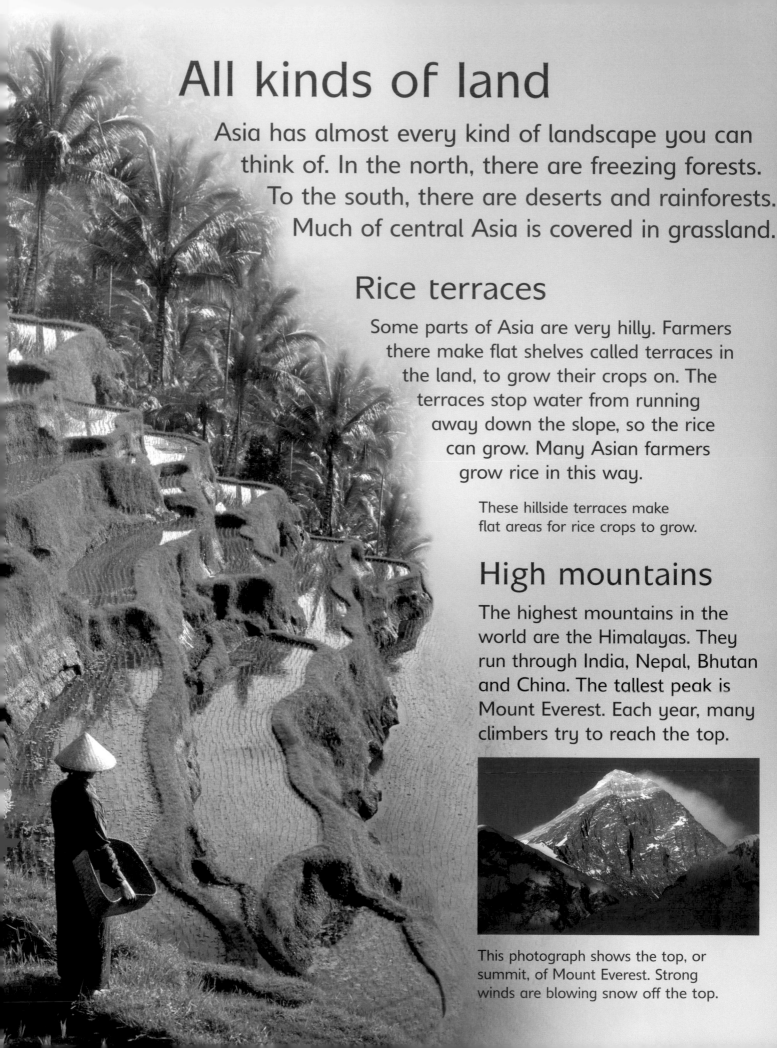

All kinds of land

Asia has almost every kind of landscape you can think of. In the north, there are freezing forests. To the south, there are deserts and rainforests. Much of central Asia is covered in grassland.

Rice terraces

Some parts of Asia are very hilly. Farmers there make flat shelves called terraces in the land, to grow their crops on. The terraces stop water from running away down the slope, so the rice can grow. Many Asian farmers grow rice in this way.

These hillside terraces make flat areas for rice crops to grow.

High mountains

The highest mountains in the world are the Himalayas. They run through India, Nepal, Bhutan and China. The tallest peak is Mount Everest. Each year, many climbers try to reach the top.

This photograph shows the top, or summit, of Mount Everest. Strong winds are blowing snow off the top.

Rainy seasons

India has two main seasons. One is very rainy, and the other is very dry. These changing seasons are caused by the way the wind blows, and are called monsoons. The monsoons affect when crops can grow.

In winter, monsoon winds blow from the land out to sea. This is the dry season.

In summer, monsoon winds blow in from the sea, bringing rain. This is the wet season.

Great Wall of China

The people of China built an amazing wall hundreds of years ago, to protect their country from enemies. The Great Wall of China passes through deserts, mountains and grasslands along the northern edge of China.

Internet links

For links to websites with photographs of views of some amazing sights in Asia, go to **www.usborne.com/quicklinks**

The Great Wall of China is made of stone. These watch-towers helped soldiers see their enemies coming.

Many ways of life

Some areas of Asia have hardly any people living in them, but others are very crowded. People across Asia have lots of different beliefs and customs. Ancient traditions often survive alongside modern ways of life.

Tallest buildings

The Petronas Towers in Kuala Lumpur, the capital city of Malaysia are among the tallest buildings in the world. They are 452m (1,438ft) high, and have 88 floors, which are used for offices.

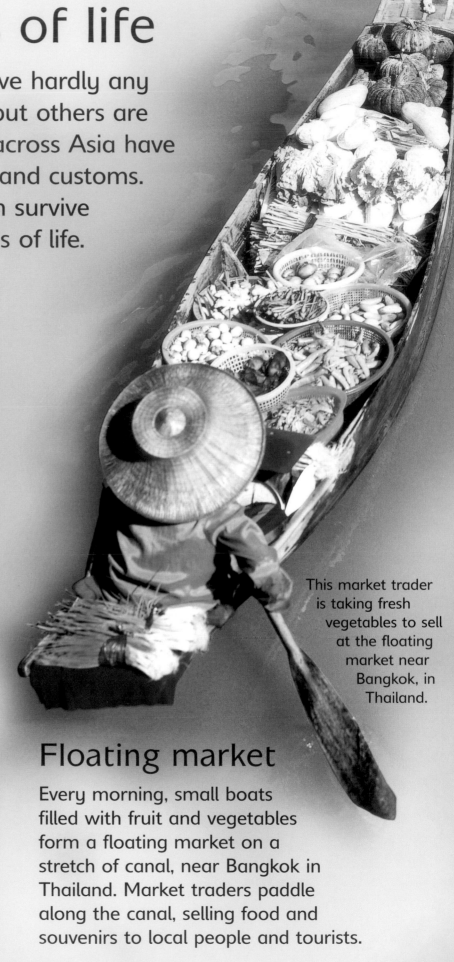

This market trader is taking fresh vegetables to sell at the floating market near Bangkok, in Thailand.

The Petronas Towers are much taller than other skyscrapers nearby.

Floating market

Every morning, small boats filled with fruit and vegetables form a floating market on a stretch of canal, near Bangkok in Thailand. Market traders paddle along the canal, selling food and souvenirs to local people and tourists.

Crowded country

China has the biggest population of any country. Over one-fifth of all the people in the world live there. Most of them live in big cities, though. In some parts of China, there are no people at all.

Internet links

For links to websites where you can find out about the everyday lives of people across Asia, go to **www.usborne.com/quicklinks**

Key
people in each km² (0.39 sq miles)

None (deserts)

Fewer than 1

Up to 100

More than 100

This map shows where most people live in China.

Glittering spires

Many of the world's religions started in Asia. Buddhism began in India and spread to other Asian countries, including Burma. There are many Buddhist temples in Burma. They are often decorated with pointed spires and large gold statues.

These golden spires are part of a Buddhist temple in Mandalay, Burma.

ATLANTIC

OCEAN

Mediterranean Se

Algiers • Tunis

Oran

Casablanca • Rabat

MOROCCO   **TUNISIA**

Marrakech ∘   *Atlas Mountains*   Tripoli

Bengha

Madeira
(Portugal)

Canary Islands
(Spain)

ALGERIA   **LIBYA**

S A H A R A   D E S E R

Laayoune ▪   *Ahaggar*
Mountains

Tropic of Cancer

Tibesti
Mountains

WESTERN
SAHARA
(Morocco)

MAURITANIA   **MALI**   **NIGER**   **CHAD**

Nouakchott ▪

Senegal   Tombouctou
(Timbuktu) ∘   *S a h e l*   *Lake Chad*

CAPE VERDE ∘   Dakar   Niamey ▪   Ndjamena ▪

Praia ▪   **SENEGAL**   Bamako ▪   *Niger*
Banjul ▪   ∘ Kano

THE GAMBIA   Bissau ▪   **BURKINA FASO**   **NIGERIA**   **CEN**
                                                                                      AFR
GUINEA-BISSAU   **GUINEA**   **BENIN**   Abuja ▪   **REPI**

Conakry ▪   **TOGO**   *Niger*   Bangui ▪

Freetown ▪   **IVORY**   Ouagadougou ▪
          COAST   *Lake*   Porto-Novo ▪

SIERRA LEONE   Yamoussoukro ∘ *Volta* **GHANA**   Lagos   **CAMEROON**

Monrovia ▪   Accra ▪ Lome   Malabo ▪   Yaounde ▪

LIBERIA   **EQUATORIAL**
                     GUINEA

Equator

SAO TOME   Libreville ▪ **CONGO**
AND PRINCIPE   **GABON**

Brazzaville ▪

Kinshasa ▪

ATLANTIC   Luanda ▪

OCEAN   **ANGOLA**

Benguela

Africa

Africa is the second
largest continent, and
the hottest. It stretches
from the Mediterranean
Sea in the north, across
the equator, and far
into the southern
hemisphere.

Key to Africa map

▪ Capital city

∘ Major city or town

— Border (where one country
   joins another one)

— River

▭ Coast

NAMIBIA

Namib Desert

Tropic of Capricorn   Walvis Bay ▪ Windh

Kal
De

Internet links

For links to websites where
you can print out maps and
explore African countries, go to
www.usborne.com/quicklinks

Scale

| 0km | 1,000km |
| 0 miles | 620 miles |

Orang

Cape Town ▪
Cape of Good Hope

The sandy brown areas on this satellite picture show how much of Africa is desert. The Sahara Desert is at the top of the continent.

Map labels

Alexandria
Cairo
Suez
Nile
EGYPT
yan
ert
Jawf
Aswan
Lake Nasser
Tropic of Cancer
Port Sudan
Red Sea
ERITREA
Asmara
Khartoum
Blue Nile
SUDAN
El Obeid
Lake Tana
DJIBOUTI • Djibouti
Ethiopian
Highlands
• Addis Ababa
SOUTH SUDAN
Juba
ETHIOPIA
SOMALIA
Lake Turkana
Mogadishu
Equator
Kisangani
Kampala
UGANDA
KENYA
Lake Victoria
Kigali
Nairobi
CONGO
Bujumbura
RWANDA
Mwanza
MOCRATIC
BURUNDI
Kilimanjaro
Mombasa
PUBLIC)
Lake Tanganyika
Dodoma
Victoria
Dar es Salaam
SEYCHELLES
TANZANIA
INDIAN
Lubumbashi
COMOROS
Moroni
Lake Nyasa (Lake Malawi)
OCEAN
Ndola
Lilongwe
ZAMBIA
Zambezi
Lusaka
MALAWI
Lake Kariba
Nampula
Harare
MOZAMBIQUE
Toamasina
ZIMBABWE
Beira
Antananarivo
Bulawayo
MADAGASCAR
MAURITIUS
Port Louis
TSWANA
Reunion (France)
Tropic of Capricorn
borone
Pretoria (Tshwane)
Maputo
annesburg
Mbabane
Lobamba **SWAZILAND**
oemfontein
Maseru
LESOTHO
TH
Durban
ICA
Drakensberg
Port Elizabeth
Mozambique Channel

Africa facts

Total land area 30,311,690km² (11,703,409 sq miles)

Biggest country Algeria 2,381,740km² (919,595 sq miles)

Smallest country Seychelles 455km² (176 sq miles)

Biggest island Madagascar 587,713km² (226,917 sq miles)

Highest mountain Kilimanjaro, Tanzania 5,895m (19,241ft)

Longest river River Nile, from Burundi to Egypt 6,671km (4,145 miles)

Biggest lake Lake Victoria, Tanzania 69,215km² (26,724 miles)

Highest waterfall Tugela Falls, South Africa 610m (2,001ft)

Biggest desert Sahara 9,100,000km² (3,513,530 sq miles)

This lion's sandy brown coat helps it blend in with its surroundings in its dry African grassland home.

Vast desert

A large part of Africa is covered by the Sahara, the biggest desert in the world. It's very hot there during the day, but at night the temperature often drops below freezing.

Dry desert

Hardly any rain falls in the Sahara Desert. The driest part is in Libya, where the desert is sandy. The wind blows the sand into huge piles called dunes, that form dramatic, curving shapes.

This map shows the different kinds of landscapes in Africa.

Sahara Desert

Key

● Highlands

● Scrub

○ Desert

● Rainforest

○ Savannah grasslands

Internet links

For links to websites about the different landscapes of Africa and the animals that live there, go to **www.usborne.com/quicklinks**

One of the best ways to cross the Sahara Desert is by camel. Camels can go a long time without water.

Thick rainforest

Some places in Africa have plenty of rain. The island of Madagascar is covered in thick, green rainforest. Many unusual animals, such as small, furry lemurs, live there.

Grassy plains

Large parts of Africa are hot grasslands called savannah. It's too dry there for many trees to grow, but there is enough rain for grasses. Savannah animals include lions, giraffes, elephants and zebras.

Ring-tailed lemurs live in the rainforests of Madagascar.

These zebras live in the savannah grasslands. The distant mountain is Kilimanjaro.

Farms and cities

Many people in Africa live in villages and work on farms. But now more and more people are moving to big cities to work and live.

This map shows the farming areas of Africa.

This is the Sahara Desert. No crops can grow here.

Thick rainforest

Key

● Farmland for crops and animals
○ Land not used for farming

This Zulu woman is carrying water in a clay pot.

Not enough water

Many parts of Africa don't get much rain. When there is too little rain, crops can't grow and people don't have enough water. This is called a drought. Sometimes, water may be carried or brought in pipes to a village where there is a drought.

Internet links

For links to websites about everyday life in different African countries, go to **www.usborne.com/quicklinks**

Farming for money

There are farms in most parts of Africa. Some grow grains such as corn or millet for people living nearby to eat. Others grow crops such as coffee or cocoa, to sell to other countries.

Selling crops is a good way for a country to make money. But it may mean that the people can't grow enough food to eat themselves.

This man is picking tea in Burundi. The dried leaves will be sold to countries far away.

Growing city

Cape Town is one of the three capital cities of South Africa. It is built on flat land, close to the Atlantic Ocean, around the base of Table Mountain. Cape Town is a growing city. More and more people are moving there from the countryside to find better places to live and work.

This is Cape Town, in South Africa. The nearby mountain is covered in cloud.

37

Europe

Europe is a small continent, but it has many countries in it. Only the part of Russia west of the Ural Mountains is in Europe – the rest is in Asia.

Europe is home to many types of birds, such as this common European kingfisher.

ARCTIC OCEAN

Arctic Circle

Reykjavik
ICELAND

Norwegian Sea

SWEDEN

NORWAY
Bergen
Oslo
Stockholm
Lake Vaner
Gothenburg

British Isles

Edinburgh

North Sea

Belfast

DENMARK
Copenhagen
Baltic Se

IRELAND
Dublin
UNITED KINGDOM

Gdansk

Cardiff
London

Amsterdam   Hamburg
Berlin
NETHERLANDS
The Hague
Brussels
BELGIUM   **GERMANY**   **POLAN**
Rhine   *Elbe*   *Oder*

ATLANTIC

OCEAN

English Channel

LUXEMBOURG
Luxembourg   Prague

Seine   **CZECH REPUBLIC**
Paris

Nantes   *Danube*   Munich   Vienna   Bratislav

Loire   **FRANCE**   Ber n   **LIECHTENSTEIN**   **AUSTRIA**   Budapest

SWITZERLAND   Vaduz

Bay of Biscay   Lyon   *The Alps*   **SLOVENIA**   Zagreb
Bordeaux   Milan   Ljubljana
Turin   **CROATIA**
Po
BOSNIA AND HERZEGOVINA

Bilbao   Andorra la Vella   **MONACO**   **SAN MARINO**   Sarajevo

Oporto   **ANDORRA**   Marseille   **MONTENEGR**

PORTUGAL   *Corsica (France)*   **ITALY**   Podgori

Madrid   Rome   **VATICAN CITY**   **ALBA**

Lisbon   *Tagus*   Barcelona   Tirar

SPAIN

Cordoba   Valencia   *Sardinia (Italy)*

Naples

Gibraltar (U.K.)   *M e d i t e r r a n e a n*

Sicily (Italy)

MALTA   Valletta   *Sea*

Key to Europe map

- ■ Capital city
- ○ Major city or town
- Border (where one country joins another one)
- River
- Coast

Scale

0km — 500km
0 miles — 310 miles

North Cape

Barents Sea

Murmansk

*Kola
Peninsula*

Pechora

Ural Mountains

**The rest
of Russia
is in Asia.**

Ukhta

I s l a n d

Oulu

Arkhangelsk

Northern Dvina

FINLAND

Lake Onega

R U S S I A

Perm

Lake Ladoga

inki

St. Petersburg

Cherepovets

Kama

Tallinn

*Rybinsk
Reservoir*

Volga

ESTONIA

Nizhniy Novgorod

Kazan

iga

LATVIA

Samara

Moscow

Tula

THUANIA

Vilnius

Don

Minsk

Volga

BELARUS

Voronezh

aw

Kiev

Kharkiv

Volgograd

Dnieper

UKRAINE

Donetsk

Volga

Lviv

Astrakhan

AKIA

Dnipropetrovsk

Don

Carpathian Mountains

Rostov

tula

w

MOLDOVA

*Sea of
Azov*

*Caspian
Sea*

GARY

Chisinau

Cluj-Napoca

Odesa

*Crimean
Peninsula*

ROMANIA

Caucasus Mountains

rade

Bucharest

Mount Elbrus

Danube

Black Sea

BIA

Bucharest

stina

BULGARIA

OVO

Sofia

Skopje

ACEDONIA

EECE

*Aegean
Sea*

Athens

*Crete
(Greece)*

Arctic Circle

Europe facts

Total land area 10,180,000km²
(3,930,520sq miles)

Biggest country Russia
Total area: 17,075,200km²
(6,592,772 sq miles)
Area of European Russia:
4,294,400km² *(1, 658,077 sq miles)*

Smallest country Vatican City
0.44km² *(0.17 sq miles)*

Biggest island Great Britain
209,331km² *(80,823 sq miles)*

Highest mountain Mount Elbrus,
Russia 5,642m *(18,510ft)*

Longest river Volga 3,692km
(2,294 miles)

Biggest lake Lake Ladoga, Russia
17,700km² *(6,834 sq miles)*

Highest waterfall Utigard, on
the Jostedal Glacier, Norway
800m *(2,625ft)*

Biggest desert There are no
deserts in Europe.

Internet links

For links to websites where
you can find maps to print
and activities about Europe, go to
www.usborne.com/quicklinks

This satellite photograph
shows how Europe joins
onto Asia. The big, white
patch at the top is the ice
that covers the Arctic.

Farms and hills

A lot of the land in Europe is gently hilly and good for farming. Some areas are rocky or snowy, and fewer crops grow there.

This map shows some of the crops that grow in Europe.

Key

● Grapes

● Olives (for oil)

● Fruit

● Potatoes

○ Grains, such as wheat and barley

Europe

Asia

Mediterranean Sea

Fruit and vegetables

The south of Europe is on the coast of the Mediterranean Sea. The weather there is very hot and dry in summer, but cool and wet in winter. Oranges, lemons and other citrus fruits grow well there, as well as many other kinds of fruit and vegetables.

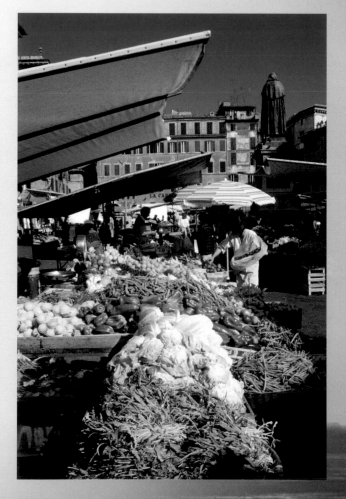

This market is in Rome, in Italy. Every day, people bring fresh fruit and vegetables from the farms nearby, to sell at the market.

Natural hot water

The island of Iceland has natural hot water, heated by rocks under the Earth. From time to time, jets of steam and hot water burst out through holes in the ground. These jets are called geysers.

This is Strokkur Geyser, in Iceland. Boiling hot water erupts from it every few minutes.

Jagged peaks

The largest group of mountains in Europe is the Alps. They formed millions of years ago, out of giant folds of rock. They have very jagged shapes, which were carved out by rivers of ice, called glaciers.

This picture shows how some of the valleys and lower slopes of the Alps are used for farming crops. Behind, you can see much higher, snowy peaks.

Internet links

For links to websites where you can discover the foods and traditions of European countries, go to **www.usborne.com/quicklinks**

Places to see

Europe is famous for its beautiful old cities and historic buildings. But many exciting modern buildings attract visitors too.

Eiffel Tower

The Eiffel Tower was built in 1889, in Paris, the capital city of France. Until 1930, it was the tallest tower in the world. Since it was built, more than 200 million people have visited it.

The Eiffel Tower in France is as tall as over 100 trucks stacked on top of each other.

Great cathedrals

Many cities in Europe have huge churches called cathedrals. They are made of carved stone, and took many years to build. Some have pointed spires on top, others have towers or rounded domes.

This is Cologne Cathedral in Germany. It took 600 years to build.

Modern buildings

There are some amazing modern buildings in Europe. One of the most interesting is Spain's Museo Guggenheim Bilbao. It is covered with huge curving sheets of metal.

This is the Museo Guggenheim Bilbao in Spain. It is a gallery where people go to look at modern art.

Roman remains

About 2,000 years ago, Rome was one of the biggest cities in the world. At that time, the Romans ruled all the lands around the Mediterranean Sea. Ruins of Roman buildings can still be seen in lots of places in Europe.

Internet links

For links to websites with virtual tours of Europe's historic buildings, go to **www.usborne.com/quicklinks**

This map shows where the Romans ruled in Europe. These lands were called the Roman Empire.

Europe

Rome

Asia

These are the remains of the Colosseum in Rome. People came here to see fighters called gladiators.

Key

● The Roman Empire

Oceania

Oceania is the smallest continent. It is made up of Australia, New Zealand and Papua New Guinea, as well as many smaller islands dotted across the Pacific Ocean.

Northern Mariana Islands
(U.S.A.)

Guam (U.S.A.)

M i c r o n e s i a

MARSHALL ISLANDS

Melekeok ■

Palikir ■

Majuro ■

PALAU

**FEDERATED STATES
OF MICRONESIA**

Bairiki ■

Equator

Yaren ■

NAURU

New Ireland

PAPUA NEW GUINEA

M e l a n e s i a

New Guinea

▲ *Mount Wilhelm*

New Britain

Port
Moresby ■

**SOLOMON
ISLANDS**

TUVA

Funafuti ■

*Arafura
Sea*

Torres Strait

Honiara ■

*Timor
Sea*

Darwin ○

*Gulf of
Carpentaria*

Great Barrier Reef

*Coral
Sea*

VANUATU

Wal
Fu
(Fr

*INDIAN
OCEAN*

Cairns ○

Vanua Levu

Port Vila ■

Viti Levu Suv

Great Sandy Desert

AUSTRALIA

Great Dividing Range

New Caledonia
(France)

Noumea ○

FIJI

Tropic of Capricorn

Alice Springs ○

▲ *Uluru (Ayers Rock)*

Great Victoria Desert

Darling

Brisbane ○

*Great
Australian Bight*

Perth ○

Adelaide ○

Murray

Sydney ○

Canberra ■

Melbourne ■

Auckland ○

North Island

Bass Strait

*Tasman
Sea*

**NEW
ZEALAND**

Wellington ■

Tasmania

Christchurch ○
South Island

Key to Oceania map

- ■ Capital city
- ○ Major city or town
- — River
- ▨ Coast

Scale

0km   1,000km
0 miles   620 miles

Oceania facts

Total land area 8,564,400km²
(3,306,733 sq miles)

Biggest country Australia 7,741,220km²
(2,988,902 sq miles)

Smallest country Nauru 21km² (8 sq miles)

Biggest island New Guinea 785,753km²
(303,381 sq miles)

Highest mountain Mount Wilhelm,
Papua New Guinea 4,509m (14,793ft)

Longest river Murray/Darling River Australia
3,718km (2,310 miles)

Biggest lake Lake Eyre, Australia 9,500km²
(3,668 sq miles)

Highest waterfall Sutherland Falls on the
Arthur River, New Zealand 580m (1,903ft)

Biggest desert Great Victoria Desert, Australia
388,500km² (150,001 sq miles)

P o l y n e s i a

Equator

PACIFIC OCEAN

KIRIBATI

Tokelau
(New Zealand)

AMOA
Apia

American Samoa
(U.S.A.)

Cook Islands
(New Zealand)

GA

Niue
(New Zealand)

alofa

Tahiti

French Polynesia
(France)

Tropic of Capricorn

Pitcairn Islands
(U.K.)

International Date Line

Some of the countries in
Oceania are made up of hundreds
of islands, which are too small to
be seen on this map. The red lines
show where one country ends and
another begins.

This photograph was taken from
space. The light brown areas
show that much of Australia is
desert. The large, white area
below Australia is Antarctica.

Wallabies live
in the dry, dusty
grasslands of
Australia. Their long
eyelashes protect
their eyes from
blowing sand.

Internet links

For links to websites with maps
to print and video tours of
countries in Oceania, go to
www.usborne.com/quicklinks

Desert and ocean

Oceania is made up of over 20,000 islands in the Pacific Ocean. Most of them are tiny, but the desert land of Australia is huge. Many small islands are the tops of underwater volcanoes.

The deepest place

The bottom of the Pacific Ocean is covered in mountains, and valleys called trenches. The deepest place on Earth is in the Mariana Trench. It is over 11km (6.8 miles) deep. If you dropped a small rock into the sea, it would take over an hour to reach the bottom of the Mariana Trench.

These maps show the Mariana Trench and the Challenger Deep, which is its deepest part.

Japan (Asia)

Philippines (Asia)

Mariana Islands

Mariana Islands (enlarged)

Guam

Key

Islands

Trench

Challenger Deep

Ancient land

Most of Australia is a bare, rocky desert. Its land has hardly changed for millions of years. The rocks have slowly been worn into smooth shapes by the wind and rain.

Wave Rock in Australia looks like a towering wall of water. It was worn into this unusual shape by the wind and rain.

Internet links

For links to websites with photos and activities about Pacific islands, go to
www.usborne.com/quicklinks

How islands form

The oldest islands in Oceania are made of limestone rock. The youngest islands are the tips of underwater volcanoes. These pictures show how an island forms and changes.

A volcano grows under the sea and rises up above the surface. When it stops erupting, animals and plants live on it.

Sea animals called corals grow around the edge of the dead volcano. They form a ring of coral called an atoll.

The coral dies and forms hard limestone. Forests grow on these new islands. The soft rock of the volcano is slowly worn away by the sea.

The middle part of this island in French Polynesia is a volcano. It is surrounded by coral reefs, which are large areas of tiny sea animals called corals.

Forests by the sea

Mangrove trees live on the edge of warm seas, with their roots partly underwater. Unlike most plants, they aren't harmed by salty sea water. Thick mangrove forests grow in Papua New Guinea and other islands in Oceania.

The roots of mangrove trees spread out wide and prop the trees up in the swampy ground.

Ocean living

Fewer people live in Oceania than on any other continent apart from Antarctica. Most of Oceania's people live near the sea.

Australia's people

Four out of five Australians live in towns and cities that are within one hour's drive of the sea. The rest live scattered across the huge desert area called the outback. People there live so far apart that some children have to do their schoolwork by mail or over the internet.

This map shows how many people live in different parts of Australia.

Most Australians live near the sea, and many enjoy water sports. This man has found a good wave to surf, near a beach in Australia.

Original people

Most people in Australia and New Zealand today are related to people who came from Europe. But the first people in Australia were the Aboriginal people, thousands of years before. The first settlers in New Zealand were the Maoris.

Key
people in each
km² (0.39 sq miles)

● More than 50

● 4–50

○ 2–4

○ 1–2

○ Fewer than 1

These men are wearing traditional Maori costumes. All children in New Zealand learn about Maori traditions at school.

Internet links

For links to websites about the Aboriginal people of Australia and the Maori of New Zealand, go to **www.usborne.com/quicklinks**

Fiji's farmers

Many Fijians are farmers. They grow enough food, such as corn and vegetables, for their families and other people in their villages. Some of their crops, such as coconuts and sugar cane, are sold to other countries.

Farming people on Fiji often live in one-room houses like these, with thatched roofs and woven floor mats inside.

Dressing up

The Huli people live in the mountains of Papua New Guinea. Huli men paint their faces and dress in spectacular feathered wigs to perform dances, which are famous all over the world.

This Huli man is putting on face paint. His wig is made from grasses, and feathers from a bird called a cassowary.

The Arctic

The area around the North Pole is called the Arctic. There's no land at the North Pole, but the sea there is so cold that its surface freezes and turns to thick ice.

The white patch on this globe shows the parts of the Arctic that are always covered with ice.

Frozen land

The Arctic Circle is an imaginary line around the Arctic. Eight countries have land inside the Arctic Circle. This land is called tundra. The soil there is frozen for most of the year. No trees can grow, but lichen and moss plants grow close to the ground.

Internet links

For links to websites where you can learn more about animals that live in the Arctic, go to **www.usborne.com/quicklinks**

Coping with cold

Arctic animals have to survive freezing temperatures. Many have thick, bushy white coats to keep them warm and help them blend in with the snow. Some have a layer of fat for extra warmth.

This baby harp seal has thick fur, and a layer of fat under its skin to keep it warm.

Scale

0km	1,000km
0 miles	620 miles

PACIFIC

OCEAN

Aleutian Islands

Bering
Sea

JAPAN
○ Sapporo

○ Petropavlosk-
Kamchatskiy

○ Anchorage

○ Anadyr

ALASKA
(U.S.A.)

Arctic Circle

RUSSIA

Chukchi
Sea

Rocky Mountains   Yukon

Wrangel
Island

East
Siberian
Sea

Verkhoyansk Range

Beaufort
Sea

New
Siberia
Islands

Lena

○ Yellowknife

Laptev
Sea

Victoria
Island

Queen

North
Magnetic Pole
+

Elizabeth
Islands

Severnaya
Zemlya

CANADA

ARCTIC

Yenisey

+ North Pole

Ellesmere
Island

OCEAN

Baffin
Island

Kara
Sea

Baffin
Bay

Franz
Josef
Land

Novaya
Zemlya

Davis Strait

GREENLAND
(Denmark)

Svalbard
(Norway)

Ob

Ural Mountains

Barents
Sea

RUSSIA

○ Yekaterinburg

■ Nuuk

Greenland
Sea

○ Murmansk

○ Arkhangelsk

Norwegian
Sea

Arctic Circle

■ Reykjavik

FINLAND

○ Nizhniy
Novgorod

ICELAND

■ Helsinki

Key to Arctic map

- ■ Capital city
- ○ Major city or town
- ▬ Border (where one country joins another one)
- ─ River
- ▬ Coast

Faroe
Islands
(Denmark)

SWEDEN

ESTONIA

ATLANTIC

NORWAY

■ Stockholm

■ Moscow

Baltic
Sea

LATVIA

OCEAN

Oslo ■

LITHUANIA

RUSSIA

BELARUS

North
Sea

DENMARK

POLAND

UKRAINE

IRELAND

UNITED
KINGDOM

GERMANY

MOLDOVA

NETHERLANDS

CZECH

SLOVAKIA

Black Sea

The Antarctic

The Antarctic, also called Antarctica, is the continent at the South Pole. It is the coldest and windiest continent. The land is covered with ice over 2,000m (6,500ft) thick. Nine-tenths of all the world's ice is in the Antarctic.

The Antarctic is at the bottom of the Earth. It is surrounded by the Southern Ocean.

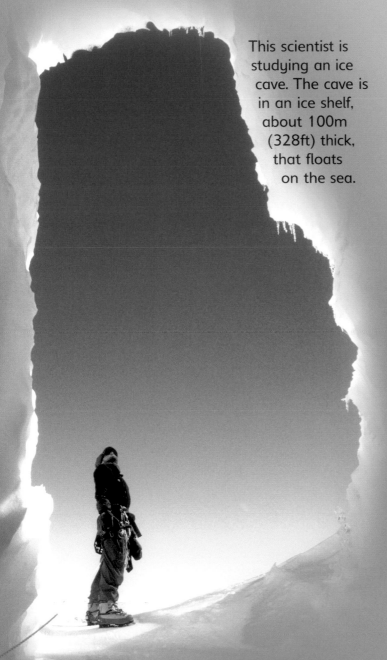

This scientist is studying an ice cave. The cave is in an ice shelf, about 100m (328ft) thick, that floats on the sea.

Home for scientists

People started exploring the Antarctic just over 100 years ago. The only people who live there today are scientists. They study the weather, ice and rocks to try to find out more about life on Earth.

Keeping warm

The Antarctic is home to thousands of penguins. They have layers of fat underneath their feathers to protect them from the cold, and huddle together in big groups for extra warmth. Penguins take turns standing at the edge of the group, where it's windy and much colder.

Internet links

For links to websites about life in the Antarctic, with video clips and satellite views, go to **www.usborne.com/quicklinks**

South Georgia
(U.K.)

South Sandwich
Islands
(U.K.)

Antarctic Circle

South Orkney Islands
(U.K.)

South Shetland Islands
(U.K.)

Queen Maud Land

Antarctic
Peninsula

*Weddell
Sea*

Coats
Land

Enderby
Land

ANTARCTICA

*East
Antarctica*

*Ronne
Ice Shelf*

*Bellingshausen
Sea*

Vinson Massif
▲
5,140m
(16,863ft)

*Ellsworth
Land*

+ South Pole

Transantarctic Mountains

*West
Antarctica*

Marie Byrd Land

*Amundsen
Sea*

*Ross
Ice Shelf*

Wilkes Land

Ross Sea

*Victoria
Land*

South Magnetic
Pole
+

Antarctic Circle

Scale

0km	1,000km
0 miles	620 miles

Key to Antarctic map

▲ Mountain

▨ Coast

This emperor penguin chick is
keeping warm by standing on
its mother's feet and snuggling
up against her tummy.

Flags of the world

North America

 Antigua and Barbuda

 Bahamas

 Barbados

 Belize

 Canada

 Costa Rica

 Cuba

 Dominica

 Dominican Republic

 El Salvador

 Grenada

 Guatemala

 Haiti

 Honduras

 Jamaica

 Mexico

 Nicaragua

 Panama

 St. Kitts and Nevis

 St. Lucia

 St. Vincent and the Grenadines

 Trinidad and Tobago

 United States of America

South America

 Argentina

 Bolivia

 Brazil

 Chile

 Colombia

 Ecuador

 Guyana

 Paraguay

 Peru

 Suriname

 Uruguay

 Venezuela

Asia

 Afghanistan

 Armenia

 Azerbaijan

 Bahrain

 Bangladesh

 Bhutan

 Brunei

 Burma (Myanmar)

 Cambodia

 China

 East Timor

 Georgia

Asia (continued)

 India

 Indonesia

 Iran

 Iraq

 Israel

 Japan

 Jordan

 Kazakhstan

 Kuwait

 Kyrgyzstan

 Laos

 Lebanon

 Malaysia

 Maldives

 Mongolia

 Nepal

 North Korea

 Oman

 Pakistan

 Philippines

 Qatar

 Russian Federation

 Saudi Arabia

 Singapore

 South Korea

 Sri Lanka

 Syria

 Tajikistan

 Thailand

 Turkey

 Turkmenistan

 United Arab Emirates

 Uzbekistan

 Vietnam

 Yemen

Africa

 Algeria

 Angola

 Benin

 Botswana

 Burkina Faso

 Burundi

 Cameroon

 Cape Verde

 Central African Republic

 Chad

 Comoros

Congo

 Congo (Democratic Republic)

 Djibouti

 Egypt

Equatorial Guinea

Eritrea

 Ethiopia

Africa (continued)

 Gabon

 The Gambia

 Ghana

 Guinea

 Guinea-Bissau

 Ivory Coast

 Kenya

 Lesotho

 Liberia

 Libya

 Madagascar

 Malawi

 Mali

 Mauritania

 Mauritius

 Morocco

 Mozambique

 Namibia

 Niger

 Nigeria

 Rwanda

 Sao Tome and Principe

 Senegal

 Seychelles

 Sierra Leone

 Somalia

 South Africa

 South Sudan

 Sudan

 Swaziland

 Tanzania

 Togo

 Tunisia

 Uganda

 Zambia

 Zimbabwe

Europe

 Albania

 Andorra

 Austria

Belarus

Belgium

Bosnia and Herzegovina

Bulgaria

 Croatia

 Cyprus

Czech Republic

 Denmark

 Estonia

Finland

France

Germany

Greece

Hungary

Iceland

56

Europe (continued)

Ireland

Italy

Kosovo

Latvia

Liechtenstein

Lithuania

Luxembourg

Macedonia

Malta

Moldova

Monaco

Montenegro

Netherlands

Norway

Poland

Portugal

Romania

Russian Federation

San Marino

Serbia

Slovakia

Slovenia

Spain

Sweden

Switzerland

Turkey

Ukraine

United Kingdom

Vatican City

Oceania

Australia

Federated States of Micronesia

Fiji

Kiribati

Marshall Islands

Nauru

New Zealand

Palau

Papau New Guinea

Samoa

Solomon Islands

Tonga

Tuvalu

Vanuatu

Changing flags

Flags of the world change frequently. New flags are invented as new countries are born, or their situation changes.

For example, in 1991, there were important changes to the way South Africa was run. All adults in the country were allowed to vote in free elections for the first time. To celebrate this, a new flag was designed.

South African flag until 1994

South African flag from 1994

Internet links

For links to websites with flags and facts, go to **www.usborne.com/quicklinks**

Map index

This is an index of all the places and features named on the maps. Each entry may contain the following parts: the name of the country, place or feature (in **bold** type), the country or region where a place or feature is (in *italic* type), and the page(s) where it can be found (in plain type). Some names also have a description explaining exactly what kind of place they are, for example, capital cities or rivers.

61

Index

Acknowledgements

This edition updated by Lisa Jane Gillespie and Vanessa Winch

Additional design: Adam Constantine, Michael Hill, Karen Tomlins, Joanne Kirkby, Luke Sargent and Lindsay North

Additional illustrations: Adam Larkum   Website adviser: Lisa Watts   American editor: Carrie Armstrong

Every effort has been made to trace the copyright holders of the material in this book. If any rights have been omitted, the publishers offer to rectify this in any future edition, following notification. The publishers are grateful to the following organizations and individuals for their contribution and permission to reproduce this material.

Cover Science Photo Library (tl) Louise Murray; (bl) Mike Agliolo; (br) Gary Hincks; **1** Science Photo Library/NASA; **2–3** Getty Images/Pal Hermansen; **5** Getty Images/Walter Bibikow; **7** Getty Images/Louise Murray; **8**(b) Dave G. Houser/CORBIS; **14**(bl) Digital Vision; **15**(tr) Julian Baum & David Angus/Science Photo Library; **16**(l) Getty Images/ John Giustina; **16–17** Getty Images/Macduff Everton; **17**(tr) Roger Ressmeyer/CORBIS; **18** Powerstock; **19**(tr) Owaki-Kulla/CORBIS, (bl) Friedrich Stark/Alamy, (br) Getty Images/Doug Armand; **20**(bl) Digital Vision; **21**(tr) Julian Baum & David Angus/Science Photo Library; **22** Galen Rowell/CORBIS; **23**(tl) Powerstock, (r) Owen Franken/ CORBIS, (bl) Robert Harding Picture Library Ltd/Alamy; **24** Jim Zuckerman/Alamy; **25**(r) Robert Harding Picture Library Ltd/Alamy, (l) Getty Images/Ary Diesendruck; **26**(bl) Digital Vision; **27**(tr) Julian Baum & David Angus/ Science Photo Library; **28**(l) Jon Arnold Images/Alamy, (br) Michael S. Lewis/CORBIS; **29** Miles Ertman/Masterfile; **30**(main) World Pictures, (bl) Macduff Everton/CORBIS; **31**(br) Powerstock; **33**(tr) Tom Van Sant/Geosphere Project, Santa Monica/Science Photo Library, (br) Digital Vision; **34–35**(b) Getty Images/Frans Lemmens; **35**(tr) Getty Images/Nick Garbutt, (m) NHPA/Daryl Balfour; **36** Dallas and John Heaton/Alamy; **37**(tr) Getty Images/Bruno De Hogues, (bl) Getty Images/Stephen Beer; **38**(ml) Digital Vision; **39**(br) Julian Baum & David Angus/Science Photo Library; **40**(bl) Art Kowalsky/Alamy; **40–41**(main) Jon Arnold Images/Alamy; **41**(mr) Getty Images/Wilfried Krecichwost; **42**(main) Getty Images/John Lawrence, (mr) Getty Images/Jorg Greuel; **43**(t) Powerstock, (bl) Getty Images/A & L Sinibaldi; **45**(t) Planetary Visions Ltd/Science Photo Library, (b) Digital Vision; **46**(b) Jean Paul Ferrero/Ardea London Ltd; **47**(t) Chad Ehlers/Alamy, (br) Theo Allofs/CORBIS; **48**(t) Mark A. Johnson/CORBIS, (br) Anders Ryman/CORBIS; **49**(ml) Jon Arnold Images/Alamy, (r) Wolfgang Kaehler/CORBIS; **50**(b) W. Perry Conway/ CORBIS; **52** Graham Neden, Ecoscene/CORBIS; **53**(br) Tim David/CORBIS.